ADVANCE AUSTRALIA

DELAIDE ARCAD

First published in Great Britain 1984 by Colour Library Books Ltd.
© 1984 Illustrations and text: Colour Library Books Ltd.,
    Guildford, Surrey, England.
Display and text filmsetting by Acesetters Ltd.,
    Richmond, Surrey, England.
Colour separations by Llovet, Barcelona, Spain.
Printed and bound in Barcelona, Spain.
by JISA-Rieusset and Eurobinder.
ISBN 0 86283 143 1

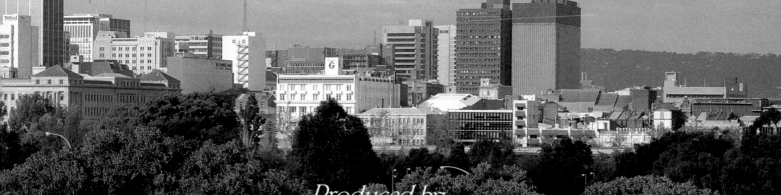

AUSTRALIA'S HERITAGE
SOUTH AUSTRALIA

Produced by
Ted Smart & David Gibbon

Published by Colour Library Books for
GORDON & GOTCH LTD

South Australia is known as the Festival State, and it did not gain its name without good reason. Everywhere the visitor turns the people seem to be celebrating something; some people celebrate when the wine is laid down, others hold a festival in honour of the almond blossom, while many indulge in a beer-drinking festival; some even indulge in a cow race at Mount Compass, but most have festivals just for fun. The whole state seems to be suffused with jollity; the state capital, Adelaide, even has a Festival Centre in case anyone runs out of things to celebrate.

But life in the state has not always been so carefree and joyful, indeed there was a time when there were no settlers in the area to feel festive about anything. In those distant days of long ago the land was populated by Aborigines, living a simple hunter-gatherer way of life similar to that enjoyed in Europe during the Stone Age. But in the year that Napoleon seized power in France, a large wooden ship, with billowing white sails and flapping colours, sailed along the coast of southern *Terra Australis*. And the Aborigines ignored it completely; as far as they were concerned it did not exist. It was only when the white men took to their longboats that the Aborigines reacted; either running for cover or preparing to attack. Making a note of this peculiar behaviour, Captain Flinders sailed on.

Flinders was on a mission to chart the southern coast of the Great Southern Continent. He had already sailed the Spencer Gulf, sighted the Flinders Ranges and coasted Yorke Peninsula, charting them with such accuracy that his maps were still in use during the Second World War. When he was off the Younghusband Peninsula, Captain Flinders came across Nicolas Baudin of the French Navy aboard the *Geographe*, who had been charting the coast from the east. Somehow, in the midst of all the painstakingly accurate charting and sounding, both of these famous cartographers managed to miss the single most important geographical feature of the southern coast; the mouth of the Murray. This oversight was to lead to one of the great explorations of Australian history.

For many years after Sydney was founded the colonists had gazed upon the Great Dividing Range and wondered what was on the other side. All they had to go on were the Aboriginal Dreamtime legends which made the interior out to be a land of monsters and demons. There was, they said, one particularly nasty water monster, known as the bunyip, but no-one really took these tales seriously. When the mountains were finally breached in the early nineteenth century, the achievement posed more questions than it answered. Flowing westwards from the mountains were dozens of rivers, some of them fairly substantial. The problem was; where did all the water go? As everyone knew, just by consulting the maps of Captain Flinders, no large river emptied into the sea along the whole southern coast. As far as the explorers could see the rivers just kept running inland, never to return.

Speculation and tales abounded: there was a vast inland lake at the heart of the continent, or there were deserts so hot that no man could survive and the mighty rivers simply evaporated. The mystery of the interior deepened even further in 1821, when the famous explorer Hamilton Hume returned from the bush claiming that he had been attacked by a bunyip.

By the late 1820s, the Governor of New South Wales, Sir Ralph Darling, was getting thoroughly fed up with it all and, in 1828, sent his military secretary into the interior. Charles Sturt, though only just turned thirty, was already a veteran of the Peninsular and North American Wars. Undaunted by the challenge, Sturt set out over the hills, only to further complicate matters by discovering even more rivers flowing inland. His next expedition, however, was more successful.

Together with a squad of soldiers and a group of convicts, Sturt set off in a whaleboat to row down the Murrumbidgee River until he found out where it went. For weeks the party followed the tortuous course of the river across vast plains, that would one day become great sheep and cattle country. After many hundreds of kilometres of rowing, portages and hardship, the party found that the river, which had now been joined by at least two other major tributaries, took a right-angled bend to the south, turning away from the interior and the possibility of an inland sea. Having proved that the vast inland river network did reach the sea, in Encounter Bay where Captain Flinders met Captain Baudin, Sturt was faced with no other alternative than of returning the way he had come. When he and his intrepid party returned they were suffering from malnutrition and utter exhaustion. With these experiences behind him, Sturt returned to Britain and wrote a book.

Ironically, the inland sea for which Sturt spent so much time searching (he returned in the 1840s on another expedition) could almost be said to exist. Scattered across the deserts north of Spencer Gulf are many 'lakes', which on the maps of the area give eastern South Australia the appearance of being half covered with water. In reality the 'lakes' of blue water are relentless salt flats, hundreds of square kilometres in extent, where the sun beats down mercilessly. Lake Eyre, the best known of the salt lakes, has only been full of water three times since white men first saw it. The surface of this lake, which is some 16 metres below sea level, is so evenly flat that it was chosen by Donald Campbell in 1964 as the site for his attempt on the world land speed record.

Meanwhile, if Sturt failed to find his inland sea, the volume that he wrote encouraged settlers and financiers with the result that colonists arrived in Gulf St Vincent in 1837 and soon established Adelaide as the continent's first 'free' colony. Great emphasis was placed on the value of family migration and of market forces in land and employment. This may, in large part, account for the success of the colony.

As soon as the settlers had landed, the surveyor-general, Colonel William Light, set to work exploring the area. One of the first places that he explored was a beautiful, lush valley to the northeast of Adelaide. The valley was covered with wild plants and flowers, so Colonel Light gave it the Spanish name for 'Hill of Roses'. Unfortunately this romantic name was lost when an early cartographer wrongly labelled the area 'Barossa', by which name it has been known ever since.

Today, the Barossa is the greatest wine-growing area in the whole of Australia, the origins of wine production being traceable back to the 1840s. In that decade a group of Lutherans arrived from Silesia to escape religious persecution. With them they brought the secret of winemaking, together with many German customs. It is for these that the Valley is most famous.

The Germans are not the only group of people to bring their culture and heritage to the state; the Cornish have come as well. One evening in the middle of the nineteenth century a shepherd, near Wallaroo, had lit a fire on which to boil his billy, when he saw a burst of green flame in the fire. No doubt this had happened many times before, but this particular shepherd knew that green flames are a sure mark of a rich copper seam in the ground. By the close of 1861 the copper rush was on.

Thousands of people came pouring into the Yorke Peninsula to take advantage of the riches in the soil, and many came from Cornwall, England. At the time the tin mining industry in Cornwall was in decline and the miners eagerly took advantage of the opportunity to use their skills and experience in a new land. For sixty years, the tall chimneys and wheelhouses stood as witnesses to the Cornish traditions and customs of the people. In its day the copper mining business was said to have saved the state from bankruptcy on more than one occasion, but in time the industry wound down. Yet the Cornish traditions and customs still continue. Pasties are a favourite treat, especially for travellers, and every other year a Cornish Festival is held to celebrate the heritage of the area's first settlers.

Another of South Australia's mineral riches is still being mined in the outback by, surprisingly enough, small concerns or even individuals. Opals were discovered in the heart of the desert, some 700 kilometres from Adelaide, at what is now called Coober Pedy, in the Stuart Ranges. The beautiful 'fire' opals of South Australia are amongst the most sought after in the world. Opals may range from dull yellow and burning red to the very rare black, all the shades being due to impurities which have been absorbed into the otherwise clear gemstone. South Australia produces about half the world's output of opals, though it is impossible to be precise, as the canny miners don't actually report all their finds to the tax man.

The seams of opal are surprisingly close to the surface, which makes life easier for the individual diggers. The great drawback to mining for opals is the terrible heat which is such a feature of the land west of Lake Cadibarrawirracanna. In the height of summer, temperatures regularly top the fifty degree centigrade mark as the burning sun beats down on the bare earth. To combat the searing climate of the area, the miners have excavated homes from the living rock. The whole region is honeycombed by corridors, living quarters, shops and streets, as well as the mining shafts and tunnels themselves. There is even a church hollowed out of the rock, deep beneath the surface. It is this unusual feature of the town which earned it its name: Coober Pedy which, in the local Aborigine dialect means 'White Fellows' Hole in the Ground'.

South Australia can boast other treasures buried beneath the surface of its deserts, though they have never become the object of a rush of miners as have the opals and copper. They are the bones of giant wombats. Thousands of years ago, when the woolly mammoth roamed Europe, a species of wombat the size of a rhinoceros strode the plains of central Australia. These plains, now desert and scrubland, were then lush grassland areas with a rich wildlife. The giant wombats, or *Diprotodons*, seem to have had a habit of throwing themselves into sticky mud and then drowning. Many of the fossilised remains belonged to animals that died in this way, perhaps that is why the *Diprotodon* is no longer with us.

There is, however, one animal roaming the outback which seems a little out of place amongst the kangaroos and wallabies; the camel. When the outback was being opened up, transport was a major problem. Many of the small mining communities and tiny farming settlements were scattered across miles of desert where a horse could die of thirst. After several years of unsuccessful struggle with the problem, the answer came in a flash. If the Asians could use camels to cross deserts, so could Australians. Hundreds of camels were imported to South Australia, together with their Afghan drivers. For decades, the camel trains snaked their way across the vast empty stretches of the outback, bringing news and supplies to the remote settlements. Perhaps the most famous of the routes was the Oodnadatta Trail from Marree through Oodnadatta to Alice Springs. For many years the 'Ghans' and their camels were virtually the only link between the outside world and Alice Springs, or Stuart as it was then known. Then, in 1929, a narrow-guage railway wound its way over the Peake and Denison Ranges to Oodnadatta and Alice Springs. Almost at once the camel trains became redundant and faded away. Today, the 'Ghan train' which replaced them has also gone, the modern road and rail links to the west taking pride of place. But the camels themselves still remain, wandering the outback where any traveller can see them.

Another foreign creature now roaming the outback as a wild and integral part of the Australian fauna is the dingo. Brought to the island continent by the Aborigines many thousands of years ago, these wild dogs quickly spread and took the place of such marsupial carnivores as the Tasmanian Wolf. Indeed, the dingo is often blamed for the extinction of this beast on the mainland. Though the Aborigines found the hunting instincts of the dingoes a great help, the sheep farmers did not appreciate their sheep-catching exploits. All-out war was declared on the dingo, a bounty was given and the animal named a pest. The battle is still raging in South Australia. It is illegal to own a dingo and anyone who manages to shoot one is more likely to be congratulated than harangued for destroying a valuable part of the environment. The continuing struggle has been responsible for one of Australia's great man-made wonders. Stretching for over 9,000 kilometres and across three states runs the great dog fence. Reputed to be the longest in the world, the dog fence is constantly patrolled by riders on the lookout for holes or damaged sections through which the dreaded dingo may creep. There can be no doubt that it is rather more successful than the rabbit fences, which seemed to stop everything but rabbits.

Running north from Marree is South Australia's legendary Birdsville Track. This important 400 kilometre route was used by drovers and mailmen alike as they traversed the deserts from Queensland into South Australia. But perhaps the most famous of its travellers was also one of the earliest. Captain Starlight pioneered the route as a means of transporting the cattle he had stolen in Queensland to the rich markets of South Australia.

Sprawling across vast reaches of the Great Victoria Desert, deep into the heart of Western

Australia, is South Australia's most famous contribution to warfare: the Woomera Weapons Testing Range. Woomera is the Aboriginal word for 'spear-throwing stick' which is as apt a name as any for a missile testing site. Long-range guided missiles are tracked across the empty desert to test their fuel and guidance systems. Established in 1947, the range has since been used to test and track space satellites belonging to the European Space Vehicle Launcher Development Organisation, known, for some obscure reason, as ELDO.

The same Colonel William Light who discovered, but failed to name, the Barossa Valley left behind him a remarkable testimony to his planning genius: Adelaide. After proclaiming the colony on 1st May 1836 under a gum tree, which still survives, the settlers got on with the mundane job of farming and surviving, while Colonel Light went off into the bush to find a site for the state capital. Some ten kilometres to the northeast of the gum tree, Colonel Light found a spot on the banks of the River Torrens which lay between the Mount Lofty Ranges and the sea. He was much taken with the site but his orders obliged him to find the *ideal* site, so once more he had to force himself to go off exploring while everyone else got on with the ploughing. As he said himself, "Although my duty obliges me to look at other places first before I fix the capital, yet I feel assured...that I would only be wasting time. This is most eligible, safe, and more beautiful than I could have hoped for." After exploring a large area of land above the Fleurieu Peninsula, Colonel Light decided that he had been right all along and got down to the serious business of planning a capital city.

It was decided to name the new town in honour of Queen Adelaide, the wife of King William IV. The original city laid out by Colonel Light has, of course, been long since outstripped by the new suburbs in both size and population, but the original plan can still be seen. Colonel Light designed a square mile of city based on a grid system of interlocking streets meeting at right angles. Within this area were placed five garden squares, in the pattern of a five of clubs, for the enjoyment of the citizens. The whole was surrounded by a half-mile wide belt of parkland which, it was declared, was "never to be built on or violated". The encircling strip of parkland has survived, giving Adelaide's citizens a beautiful facility, and the city a unique air and atmosphere. Thanks to the Colonel's great foresight, the broad streets of the city centre remain traffic-free and amongst the most beautiful in the world. A statue of the Colonel who did so much for the city is now on Montefiore Hill, overlooking his city, and is called 'Light's Vision'.

For many years the city of Adelaide, and indeed the whole of the state, had a somewhat conservative reputation of staid, olde-worlde charm. The city of Adelaide was known as the 'City of Churches', due to the large number of beautifully designed places of worship it contained. There are two cathedrals, together with a mosque, a synagogue and dozens of churches. It may equally well have been known as the 'City of Restaurants' for there are more here per head of population than in any other city in Australia, or the 'City of Pubs', there being a great number and variety of these establishments. The outskirts of the city were pictured as typical suburbia, where barbecues are held and Barossa wines passed leisurely from hand-to-hand. But some years ago the authorities decided that a change of image was needed if the state was to cash in on the tourists and migrants. So the 'Festival State' was born.

By some careful marketing techniques, the word was put out that Adelaide was a fun and trend-setting place to visit. The city authorities were not content with telling everyone that Adelaide was an exciting place, they went out of their way to make it true. The Festival Centre was built and many annual and bienniel events staged: the Christmas Pageant, the Royal Adelaide Show, the Wine and Food Frolic and the Adelaide Festival sprang up in the city itself, while outlying towns were encouraged to maintain or start local festivals.

All in all the State of South Australia is one of the most diverse and attractive in Australia. From the burning barrenness of Coober Pedy to the lush parks of Adelaide to the almost endless jollity as one festival follows another, South Australia is a place to enthral the visitor and resident alike with its beauty and atmosphere.

Previous page Adelaide's Festival Centre illuminated at dusk. *Above* the Botanic Hotel in Adelaide. *Top, right and facing page* startling vistas of the Festival Centre. Set next to the Torrens River it is home to the world-famous Adelaide Arts Festival. This is a wonderful celebration which displays the cultural excellence of the state. *Overleaf* Saint Peter's Cathedral, one of Adelaide's many churches.

Top the Governor's Residence. *Above* the gracious fountain which stands in Hindmarsh Square *left*. The square stands near the northern end of Pulteney Street *facing* *page, top. Overleaf* the city seen from Montefiore Park. On top of Montefiore Hill stands Light's Vision, a tribute to Colonel Light who planned Adelaide's layout.

These pages Rundle Mall is a unique pedestrian thoroughfare. Here can be found the main departmental stores and other major retailers. There are bright fruit carts and flower stalls, snack bars and coffee lounges, boutiques and cinemas. Buskers play on the sunny, tree-lined mall and at the eastern end can be found shops selling handicrafts, sporting goods and photographic equipment.

Overleaf Saint Peter's Cathedral, the mother church of the Church of England in South Australia.

Top the War Memorial. *Above* trams still form a clean and efficient part of Adelaide's transport system. *Right* Edmund Wright House, built in Renaissance style, is named after the architect. *Facing page* views of North Terrace, where mellow, 19th-century stone design blends with the more modern, concrete structures. *Overleaf* Hindley Street at night.

The Torrens River, *left* with a jogger and *above and top* rowers. *Facing page* bandstand. *Overleaf* the Festival Centre and other civic buildings.

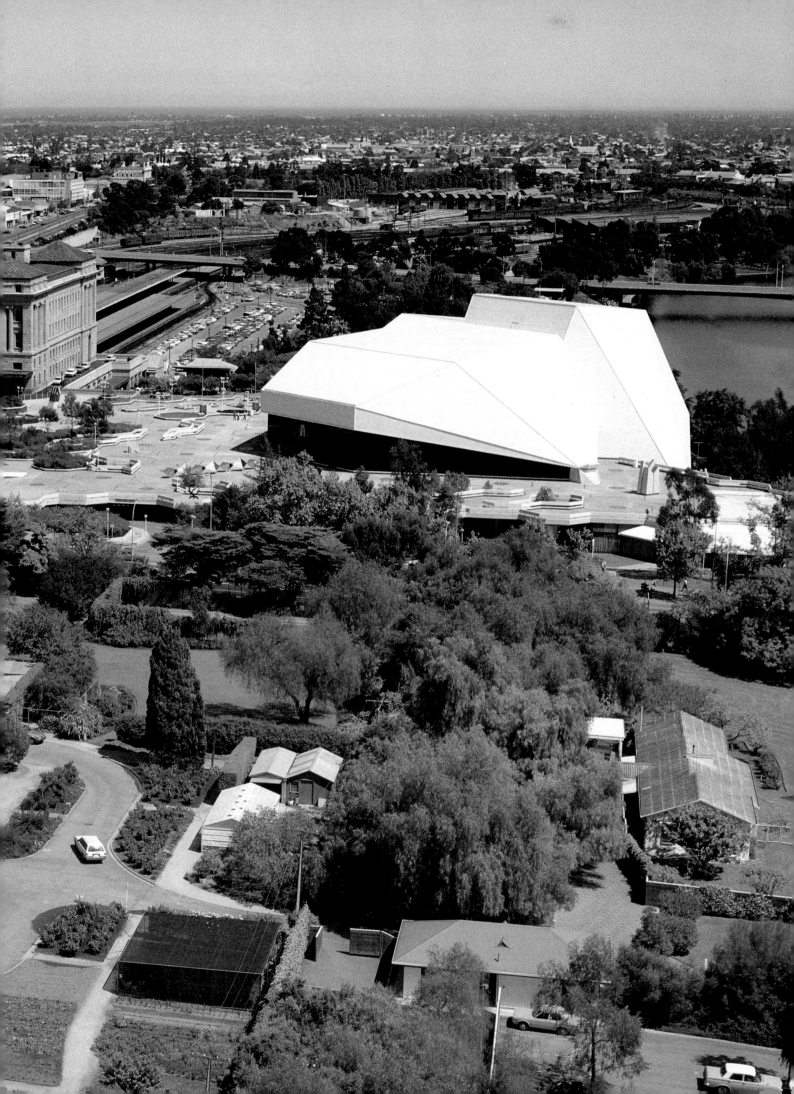

These pages Rundle Mall is a pedestrianised section of Rundle Street, between King William Street and Pulteney Street, and is one of the main shopping centres of Adelaide. The mall is packed with major stores, small boutiques, cinemas, fruit carts and snack bars. Running off Rundle Mall are a number of arcades and side-streets to explore, the whole, delightful area being very compact and colourful.

These pages and overleaf just an hour's drive north of Adelaide is the fertile Barossa Valley, which is Australia's foremost wine producing region. Although it is only 8km wide by 30km long, there is found here a lovely, quaint world of magnificent churches, imposing chateaux and tiny villages. The area was settled in the mid 19th century by Germans who had escaped religious persecution in their own country. Their cultural influence is still felt strongly today in this friendly valley.

A few kilometres from Adelaide, on the South Road, is Morphett Vale. The town contains a recreation *these pages* of a pioneer settlement of the 1860s. The reconstruction is complete with a blacksmith's *facing page, bottom,* a thatched cottage *left* and horse-drawn carriages. *Overleaf* a magnificent view across the fertile Barossa Valley, which stands on the Sturt Highway northeast of Gawler. It is here that the finest of South Australia's wines are produced.

The Barossa Valley *these pages* lies about fifty kilometres from Adelaide and enjoys a Mediterranean climate, ideal for the growth of vines *above, top and facing page* upon which the wine industry is based.

The Barossa Valley *facing page* is famed for the quality of its fruits, in particular the grapes which are used to produce the well-known wines. The valley does not, however, have a monopoly on fruit growing in South Australia. Riverland *this page* produces some two million tonnes of fruit each year, the result of successful irrigation. *Far left* lemons, *left* a fruit stall near Berri, *top left* oranges, *top right* fruit tree pruning and *above* pruning vines near Barmera.

This page the Barossa Valley: *above and top left* Tanunda, *right* near Dorrien, *centre* the Kaiser Stuhl cellars, Nuriootpa, *top right* Chateau Yaldara. *Facing page, bottom* Waikerie and *facing page, top* a Murray ferry near Berri. *Overleaf* Gawler.

Moonta *this page* is one of the towns in the 'Little Cornwall' area on the Yorke Peninsula, which boomed after the discovery of copper in 1861. Hundreds of miners from Cornwall, England, settled in the area, bringing their skills and culture. *Left* the Municipal Offices, *far left* Ellen St, *above* the Uniting Church in Australia, *above left* nearby derelict mine buildings, *top right* a miner's cottage and *top left* a house on Henry St. *Facing page, bottom* Moonta Bay and *facing page, top* nearby Port Hughes.

Wallaroo *this page* is a
port on the Yorke
Peninsula. *Top* the old
Railway Station, *left* Town
Chambers Hall and *above* the
port area. *Facing page*
Kadina, the largest town on
the Yorke Peninsula.

Port Broughton *above, right and top* is a small port on the northwest coast of the Yorke Peninsula; *facing page, top* nearby scenery. *Above right* Port Augusta *Facing page, bottom* near Port Wakefield.

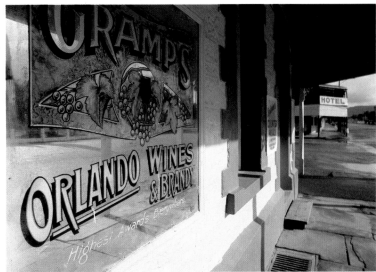

Quorn *left, above, centre left and centre right* and, further northwest, Hawker *top* are both typical, rural South Australian towns set in the Flinders Ranges and surrounded by vast areas of sheep pasture. *Facing page, bottom* Willowie Forest Reserve and *facing page, top* a view from Hancocks Lookout.

Between Lakes Torrens and Frome rise the beautiful Flinders Ranges *these pages*. The great ridges are made of tough quartzite, while the valleys are composed of softer rocks. *Top and right* the Wilpena Pound. *Above and facing page* Stokes Hill Lookout.

The Flinders Ranges are perhaps the most attractive hills in South Australia. The Flinders Ranges National Park *these pages* covers a large area of the region north of Hawker and aims at the preservation of the magnificent scenery, flora and fauna which exist in the area. *Top and facing page* the Bunyeroo Valley; *above and right* near Wilpena.

Port Augusta is a supply and communications centre for the great stretches of outback to the north. Years ago Afghans drove camels *right and facing page, top* into the interior. Today, their place has been taken by railway trains *facing page, bottom. Top* the horse racing track.

The important town of Port Augusta *these pages* lies at the head of Spencer Gulf. This town of 13,000 people is a thriving industrial centre and a major port. Its position makes it a stopping point for all east-west travellers and a vital supply base for the vast outback to the north.

The combined Town Hall and cinema *centre left* of Port Augusta was built in 1887 and stands in the same street as the buildings *remaining pictures.*

CORPORATION OF THE
CITY OF WHYALLA
BYLAW - 29

HORSES PROHIBITED
FROM FORESHORE EXCEPT
BETWEEN THE HOURS OF
5·0 AM - 9·0 AM THEN ONLY
IN A WAY WHICH IS
NOT DANGEROUS OR
INCONVENIENT TO THE PUBLIC
"PENALTY" $200.

WHYALLA CITY COUNCIL

DOG CONTROL ACT
1979 - 80

DOGS ARE PROHIBITED
FROM THE FORESHORE
UNLESS UNDER PROPER
CONTROL.

MAXIMUM PENALTY
$100

Whyalla *these pages* stands on the west shores of Spencer Gulf. With a population of over 30,000 souls it is the largest provincial city in the state. Its heavy industrial role is exemplified by the massive BHP iron and steel works, which process the ore mined further inland and brought to the city by rail. The city is also an important port and basks in a beautiful, Mediterranean-like climate.

Iron Knob *facing page, top* is a massive ore mining operation in the interior of South Australia. It is linked to Whyalla by a railway *left and facing page, bottom* across miles of scrub *above. Top* the Lincoln Highway. *Overleaf* Tumby Bay, further south.

Cowell *top, above and above left* stands on the east coast of the Eyre Peninsula. The small town lies on Franklin Harbour, an almost landlocked inlet of Spencer Gulf. Around the town are great areas of open land *remaining pictures* where a variety of livestock is grazed: *left* a camel, *facing page, top* horses and *facing page, bottom* sheep. Tumby Bay *overleaf* is a charming resort, north of Port Lincoln, which is famous for its great crescent of white sand.

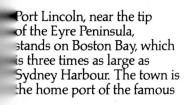

Port Lincoln, near the tip of the Eyre Peninsula, stands on Boston Bay, which is three times as large as Sydney Harbour. The town is the home port of the famous tuna fleet *facing page*. Port Lincoln Harbour *this page and overleaf* is used by both working and pleasure craft.

treaky Bay *right and top* s a growing holiday resort nd fishing town. North of he town is Perlumbie Beach *above, facing page, bottom and overleaf.* Further south is the scenic coast around Elliston *facing page, top.*

Ceduna *these pages* stands on the Great Australian Bight. With a population of over 2,000 it is the last town of any size before the Eyre Highway strikes out across the Nullarbor Plain towards Perth, hundreds of kilometres to the west. Ceduna faces the shallower waters of the Great Australian Bight where whiting is caught in great numbers. The town acts as a small port, exporting grain *below and below right* and gypsum *bottom left*. The Overseas Telecommunications Earth Station *bottom right*, which links South Australia with Asia, Africa and Europe, lies a short drive to the north. *Overleaf* the coast near Elliston.

The wild outback of western South Australia is typified *above, top and facing page, bottom* around the small town of Penong where the silo *left* is found. *Facing page, top* the coast near Port Sinclair.

Kimba is a small town of less than a thousand inhabitants, 150 kilometres southwest of Port Augusta. It serves as a centre for the surrounding sheep country, as is shown *top and right*. The Eyre Highway stretches far across the outback *facing page*. *Above* a typical outback scene near Ceduna.

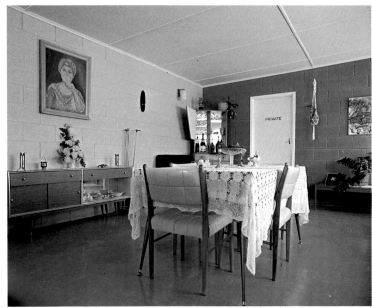

At Coober Pedy *these pages* many of the houses, stores and even churches have been cut from the solid rock.

The inhabitants of the town have been forced to live underground by the terrible heat.

Opals were discovered at Coober Pedy *these pages and overleaf* in 1911. Today, anyone armed with a permit can try their luck at finding a precious stone.